A Dictionary of Bristle

Harry Stoke & Vinny Green

◆ Tangent Books

A Dictionary of Bristle by Harry Stoke and Vinny Green first published in
2003 by Catherine Mason of Broadcast Books, second edition published
in 2006. Third Edition published by Tangent Books in 2010, Fouth edition
published 2013, this edition published 2014.

Tangent Books
Unit 5.16 Paintworks
Bristol BS4 3EH
0117 972 0645 www.tangentbooks.co.uk

978-1-906477-85-1
Copyright: Tangent Books

Publisher: Richard Jones richard@tangentbooks.co.uk
Design: Joe Burt joe@wildsparkdesign.co.uk
Production Assistant: Sol Wilkinson

This book is dedicated to

Professor Colin Pillinger, CBE (1943-2014)

Kingswood's most famous son, and the boldest, hairiest, and most determined planetary scientist Bristol has ever produced.

Introduction

Introduction

Welcome to *A Dictionary Of Bristle*: a unique collection
of words, phrases, and pronunciations that originally
started life as a simple tongue-in-cheek section from
the award-winning satirical website, *That Be Bristle*. But
from small acorns grow large trees, as is proved by the
continuing success of this Dictionary, now in its 10th
year of publication and still going strong.

Thanks to Bristolians throughout the city and around
the world, who are proud of who they are and how they
sound, we have been able to continue to update and
expand this humorous and curiously informative insight
into the strange sounding lexicon of the south west's
capital city.

In case you are not aware, Bristolian is a distinctly
warm-sounding dialect that, like most regional variations
of language, contains standard English words and
phrases that mean something very different to its native
speakers. In a city where a *drive* is somebody at the
wheel and not something you do on a Sunday afternoon,
and a *spanner* is never going to help you fix a car, life
can easily get confusing for the unwary.

Bristolian also has many words and pronunciations that
are unique to the city which can often baffle people not
familiar with the rolled Rs, the dropped Hs, and the
addition of Ls to the end of practically any word that ends

in a vowel. As if that isn't potential enough to strike a look of bewilderment onto the face of a visitor, the unaided ear also has to deal with the confusion of ownership and tense, and the use of the personal pronoun Ee (he) for impersonal objects: "*Me ammer? Ee's over yer look.*"

Like all regional dialects though, Bristolian is in danger of dying out. With the large new suburbs of Bradley Stoke and Emersons Green attracting people to Bristol from all over the UK, the 30,000+ students that fill the universities each year, and the widening of middle-class enclaves gentrifying the housing of many former working areas of the city, from Bishopston and Horfield to Easton and Southville, the melting pot of language in the city is slowly diluting Bristol's true identity.

Yet even without this slim volume to help fight its corner for the last decade, the dialect still retains its strongholds, notably in pockets of Bristol communities such as Southmead, Bedminster, Knowle West, and Hartcliffe. The language lives on, and with the help of this book and proud Bristolians everywhere, will continue to do so.

The aim of this Dictionary is to collate words and phrases in common usage in and around Bristol, both past and present, in a bid to keep the Bristolian tongue alive. Some entries in this collection cross generations and some cross over into other regional dialects and general slang, but all are listed here if they play, or have played, a part in the makeup of Bristolian. You may not recognise them all – I've been a Bristolian since birth and some still surprise even me – but with the help of this Dictionary we hope that you'll soon be hearing (and understanding) a lot more of them.

Harry Stoke

Pronunciation

A Guide To Bristolian Pronunciation And Grammar

An important test of Bristolian is that it's not only lazy in style but rhythmic as well, so that consonants are essential to achieve effortless delivery. No true Bristolian would use an iota more energy than they need to to deliver a statement. As in the morning greeting on the workers' bus – *"Awlrite 'arry?" "Awlrite, 'n thee?"* No answer is required. Elegant economy.

There are several rules to Bristolian which shape its sound and flow and are essential to master if you want to learn to speak or understand Bristolian. Its use of '**A**', '**I**', '**L**', '**R**', '**S**', '**T**', and its lack of '**H**', the pronunciation of '**TH**' and '**ING**', its confusion of ownership and tense, and its addition of words to the end of sentences. Also, harsh sounding letters and syllables are generally dropped or substituted for softer ones.

A   An '**A**' located within a word is usually pronounced like the '**a**' in Sat – a kind of drawn out '*ahh*' sound, giving words such as Apple, Glass, and Bath a distinct sound.

I   '**I**' is very often used as both a subjective and an objective personal pronoun. This turns *"Give it to me"* into *"Gif I it!"* and *"That's just like me"* into *"Thas just like I"*.

L   Words that end in a vowel often have a short '**L**' added to the end of them turning "*area*" into "*areal*" and "*idea*" into "*ideal*". This mostly occurs when the next word begins with a vowel. However, where words actually end with an '**L**' it is often silent. Where an '**L**' is pronounced it will generally be accompanied with an '**aw**' sound such as "*Breakfast Cereawl*". The letter '**L**' is also often inserted into words where the '**aw**' coupling exists such as "*drawing*" which becomes "*drawlen*".

R   '**R**' is often heavily emphasised both at the start and ending of words with the sound of '**er**', this gives them a warm tone, such as "*NeveR*", "*BabbeR*" and "*Right*".

S   '**S**' is usually added to the end of verbs when referring to all persons, instead of just the singular third person. This turns phrases like "*I go*" into "*I goes*" and "*They go*" into "*They goes*".

T   Where a '**T**' is found inside a word, it is rarely pronounced and if it is it will be very soft. This turns words like "*Westbury*" into "*Wessbree*", "*Weston*" into "*Wesson*", and even "*Bristol*" into "*Bristle*".

H	Words that begin with '**H**' are shortened disregarding the first letter giving us "*ave im*" instead of "*Have him*". This trait is also sometimes applied to the letter '**W**' as seen in "*He would*" turning into "*Ee ood*".

TH	Where the coupling of '**th**' occurs at the start of a word it will often be pronounced as an '**F**' turning "*Think*" into "*Fink*". This could also apply when it is found at the end of, or inside a word, but where this is the case it can also be pronounced as a '**D**' or a '**V**', turning "*With*" into "*Wiv*".

ING	Where the triplet of '**ing**' occurs at the end of a word it is often pronounced as '**en**' with emphasis on the '**N**', but be warned this is not always the case. Where this does occur it changes "*Going raving*?" into "*Goen rave-en*?" and "*Are you going to do all the driving*?" into "*Is you gonna do all the drive-en*?"

END   To finish a sentence generally a choice of three words can be used; '*Look*', '*Mind*', or '*See*'. Which word you use would depend upon the context of the sentence. '*Look*'; "*Yer tis, look!*" – when you find something that's been lost. '*Mind*'; "*Be careful with that, mind!*" – when you're taking a full pint back to the table in the pub. '*See*'; "*I tawld you, see!*" – when you've proved yourself right in an argument. Also when you finish a sentence part of the way through, pausing for thought, the word '*Like*' will often be inserted in the place of a more traditional 'er'; "*You can ave im fer like, a fiver or summut.*"

Dictionary

A
Of or To or The
Canave one a they?/I ain't goen back a work now.

Aarsh
Harsh
The way sheda treat ee, thas prittee bleeden aarsh!

Ackrut/Ackrutlee
Accurate/Accurately
Blige, ow ackrut do ee need a be for Christ sake; tis only a gas pipe!

Aeriawl
A particular region
What aeriawl do ee live in?

Almunsbree
A village to the north of Bristol; Almondsbury
Yeah, thas up by Almunsbree Inner Change.

Ambag
Handbag
Sheem ad er ambag nicked up Chasers. Nufink in it mind.

Amblance
Ambulance
Is diarrheawl got so bad I ad to call ee an amblance.

Americawl

United States of America
Yoom been a Disneyland? That the one in Americawl?

Amt

Have not
I amt ad me mefadone today muh, ave I?

Ank

To go fast (usually on two wheels of a four wheeled vehicle)
Ar Ole Man anked ee up the ring road. Ee beeped out as we passed Granners hearse mind.

Annall

As well
Cas ee fit I in there annall?

Annat

And that
I luvs chips, they's all spuds annat innit.

Anneye

Haven't I
I only bleeden done it again anneye!

Annum

An area east of Bristol; Hanham or Haven't they
This un go up Annum drive?

Annus Haven't we
We both gotta get that bus ohm annus?

Ansum Handsome
Eeuz evsa ansum.

Ant Has not
Ee ant even ast us what weeda want!

Anudder Another
I tawd ee I aint got annuder but ee don't lissen do ee?

Any Rate Anyway
She left I, but I dint like err any rate.

Appapie Apple pie
Ee stuck it in Ar Muh's appapie; shem up the osbidal wiv im now!

Ar Our
Ar farther, whose arts in eaven.

Ar Muh My/Our mother
Ar Muh's maken tea.

Ar Ole Man   My/Our father
Ar Ole Man bin down a pub all day.

Ard   Tough/Violent
Yooms only ard in the showers.

Ark   Look/Listen
Ark at ee.

Arrmen   As said at the end of a prayer
Ar lord, who art in Soufmeed, be nice to I. Arrmen.

Arrtack   Heart attack
Ee ad annuder arrtack up the Art Cleff Inn.

Art   Generic radio station formerly known as GWR
That art aint a same wivout Andy Bush.

Art Cleff   An area of South Bristol; Hartcliffe
Ee's sold is counsawl ows up Art Cleff. Ee don't own it mind!

Arvester

A popular grill restaurant chain;
Harvester
*Ise goen up the Arvester but ise only
avin the salad cart.*

Asdawl

A popular supermarket chain;
Asda
Ar Muh's down Asdawl at the minute.

Assant

Haven't
Ee assant gone an broke it ave ee?

Assaw

Asshole
Yer an assaw.

Assit

That's it
Assit, right yer look.

Ast

Ask or Have you
*I ast err where Asdawl waz but she
dint know/Ast ee seen me keys?*

Asthmawl

A restrictive breathing condition
*I faught it was that Darf Vader ringing
I up, but it was Ar Ole Man haven
asthmawl attack.*

Astrawl   Vauxhall Astra
I casn't get any parts for me Astrawl anymore?

At   Had
Ee at a go down ar muh's ows.

Ater   After
Cas ee look ater ee fry?

Attle Avit   Had to have it
Once ee sawl it, ee attle avit.

Ave/Avin   Have/Having
Whas wonna ave fer tea?

Aves   Has
Ee aves to go a work urrlay mind.

Avvy   To beat somebody
You could avvy – I'll old your coat!

Aw   All
Ise tellen ee – aw I ad were nine pints

Awd

Old
Ow awd are you? Yoom only looks bout elemm!

Awdin

Holding
Ee went a proper pisser awdin me glider!

Awd Ee

Hold him/this/that
Las orders? Quick awd ee while I gets anuver un in.

Awdbree Coort

Oldbury Court Estate, an area of East Bristol
They fown me car down Awdbree Coort!

Awdeez

German budget supermarket chain; Aldi
Ar Gramfer won't shop down Awdeez; summut to do wiv war.

Awlful

Awful
Them bleeden pies is awlful. Taste like a bleeden orse.

Awlrite

Are you alright
Awlrite? Ow bis?

Awlrite Me Luvver? Hello, how are you my friend?
Awlrite me luvver? Ain't seen you frages.

Awlun Common Oldland Common, an area east of Bristol
SBL? Thas down Awlun Common.

Awws All I was
Awws tryin to do was elp err!

Babby/Babber Baby or Friend
Don't be such a babby/Churz me ole babber!

Backee To carry a second person on a pushbike
Gis I a backee ohm ullee?

Baff An affluent city south east of Bristol; Bath
Iss posh out Baff mind!

Baity Riled/Annoyed
Ee was getten right baity.

Bammington A game played with shuttlecock and raquet; Badminton
I plays bammington down ar club.

Bananawls Bananas
That a bannawl in yer pocket or you just pleased to see I?

Banjo Island An area east of Bristol; Park Estate
Ave ee bin down Banjo safternun?

Bar Nil

An area of East Bristol; Barton Hill
Eda live down Bar Nil in they flats.

Barawl Gurnee

A former psychiatric hospital; Barrow Gurney
Ee's a nutter. Ee awt a be in Barawl Gurnee.

Basdurd

Bastard
Ee were a basdurd to get off I ee were.

Baws

Testicles
Ar yungun sounds like Barry White since his baws dropped.

Beamer

Going red in the face with embarrassment
Look at the gurt beamer on ee.

Bearpit

A subterranean world at the back of Debenhams
That bearpit stinks a piss mind!

Bemmie Down   An area of South Bristol that
                  overlooks the Avon Gorge.
                  *Ee cas see the spenshun bridge from
                  up Bemmie Down!*

Bemmie/Bedmie   A resident of Bedminster
                    *You ain't a true Bemmie, yoom from
                    up Wimmilill.*

Bemminser   An area of South Bristol;
                Bedminster
                *They all speaks proper down
                Bemminser mind!*

Benny   To lose your temper
            *Ee ad a right benny when I told im
            bout what sheda bin up to.*

Bide Still   Keep Still
                 Bide still ullee! Yoom doen me ead in!

Biggun   Big one
             Ee's got a gurt biggun ee ave.

Bin   Been
          Wheres ee bin wiv Ar Muh?

Birfday
Birthday
Whas get me fer me birfday then?

Bis/Bist
Are you
Ow bist our kid?

Bissen
Is not
Ee bissen gonna get nuffink out a I.

Blad
Useless idiot (derog.)
I ain't avin Stenner on my team, ee's a total blad.

Blakforn
A popular alcoholic cider drink; Dry Blackthorn
Yer, that Blakforn's bleeden luverly!

Blaze
Blaise Castle Estate, West Bristol
Ave ee seen that castle up Blaze? Iss mazen!

Bleenell
Bleeding Hell
Bleenell! I forgot miat.

Blige
Blimey
Blige! He didn't do that did ee?

Booter

When water has penetrated one's footwear following an accidental step into a puddle.
I stepped in a macky puddle goen round ar gramphers, now I got a proper booter.

Borrawl

Borrow
Can I borrawl they shoes?

Bort

Bought
I bort ee from Trade It. Like Ar Ole Man though – don't bleeden work.

Bout

About
Ave yoom erd bout what sheda been getten upto?

Bovvered

Bothered
Jew fink ise bovvered what ee wants?

Breckfuss

The first meal of the day; Breakfast
Muh, where's me breckfuss?

Bristle/Brizzle

The mother city; Bristol
We luvs Bristle!

Briz
An area of South Bristol;
Brislington
*Ee ad a right eppy when ee was in
Briz.*

Brormeed
Large shopping area in central
Bristol; Broadmead
Ar Muh got ee fry down Brormeed.

Brung
Brought
I brung me own.

Bung
Put
Jus bung it down over yer.

Burmenam
A city in the West Midlands;
Birmingham
*They all got Burmenam accents
down Brean mind.*

Buttery
A popular sandwich shed on the
harbourside; Brunel's Buttery
*Gert lush macky bacon sarnies down
a Buttery. Cas ee get I one now?*

Buzzer
Bumble Bee
*Yer gurt macky buzzer flown in me
Forn.*

Byerawl Biro
Can I borrawl yer byerawl.

Cabry Eef

An area east of Bristol; Cadbury Heath
They don't make choclut out Cabry Eef mind!

Cacks

Underwear
Thee's ad they cacks on all week.

Camrawl

Camera
Jew see they pictures on is camrawl? Proper filth!

Canadawl

Canada
Snot Americawl mind eem goen mind! Iss Canadawl!

Canave

Can I Have
Canave one a they?

Cane Shum

A small market town south east of Bristol; Keynsham
They Charity shops out Keynsham is proper smart.

Carboot Circus

Shopping centre in central Bristol; Cabot Circus
Yer, jew get they down Carboot Circus? They'm proper smart they innum?

Cas
Can
Cas ee get I one a they?

Casn't
Can not
Yer, ee casn't take pictures in Carboot Circus mind!

Caw
Coal
Do ee know if this ows is built on a caw mine?

Cawd
Cold
Cawd? Yeah, but too cawd to snow mind.

Cawlcalater
Calculator
Cas I borrawl your cawlcalater?

Chimley
Chimney
Has thee had thee chimley swept?

Chinawl
China
Yer, watch ar muh's best chinawl with that stick mind!

Choclut
Chocolate
Ee casn't rub that choclut all over I mind!

Churz

Cheers
Churz Ar Muh!

Cinemawl

Cinema
Comen down the cinemawl?

Circler

Circular
I luvs petezawls cos they'm all circler.

Cliffun

An affluent area of West Bristol;
Clifton
Iss right posh up Cliffun way mind!

Cocker

Friend
Awlrite me old cocker? Ow bis?

Colsnawl

Colston Hall
*I seen that Russell Howard down the
Colsnawl las week. Proper smart ee
were!*

Concord(e)

A supersonic Bristolian aircraft
not bought by Americans
*Ave ee seen the state a that concord
up Fill-Un? Isa bleeden disgrace!*

Cookumer

Cucumber
Muh! I dint want no cookumer wiv me salid!

Coopeyen Down

Bending over/Crouching down
I was coopeyen down and the dog bit me ass.

Coors

Of course
Coors I luvs im, ee buys I chips.

Corrie Tap

Popular cider establishment in Clifton Village; The Coronation Tap
I luvs a Corrie Tap, iss right mint fer glider.

Corried

To be deprived of normal automotive control (f. The Coronation Tap, Clifton)
That Exhibition got I right corried!

Counsawl Ows

A large building at the bottom of Park Street
Liebree? Ee's down by the Counsawl Ows me babber.

Cudda

Could of
Ee cudda told I ee was comen.

Cum off

To fall off something
I cum off me bike and got a gurt big scrage ere.

Cum Tight

Painful/To hurt
Ow you basdurd, that cum tight!

Cuntray

Country
I luvs liven in the cuntray, saul fields annat.

Custurd

Custard
Jew needs to see a doctor if tis coming out same colour as custurd.

Cyclepaff

A murderous nutter
Stay away from ee, ee's a cyclepaff!

Dap/Daps   Run/Nip or Plimsolls (Derived
from Dunlop Athletic Plimsolls)
*Eva since I bort ee those daps ees
run like Mo Fararll at Lympics.*

Dapper   A small child
*It were all better when I were a
dapper.*

Darkside   A former nightclub in Brislington;
Parkside (derog.)
*Yer thee member that right munter ee
pulled up Darkside. Shem your wife
now.*

Dats   That is
Dats a good ideawl.

Dedder/Dedun Corpse
*Yooms a dedun when Ar Ole Man
gets old of thee.*

Dees Casn't Do Dat You can't do that
Oi! Dees casn't do dat yer!

Diarrheawl   Diarrhoea
*I got diarrheawl when I was out in
Americawl.*

Diesel Gettee   You will get a punch (clench fist
whilst saying)
Diesel gettee if ee don't shut it!

Dill   Deal
*They films that Dill or No Dill up Briz,
mind.*

Dinnum   Didn't they
They made a proper mess dinnum.

Dint   Did not
I ast im but ee dint know anyfink.

Discolated   Dislocated
*Ee come off is bike and discolated is
arm.*

Disn't   Did not
Yer, I disn't say ee could ave ee!

Dissis   This is
Dissis all err stuff mind!

Do/Do's   Does
Ee do's a proper job.

Doggin Up
To look at threateningly
Ee's doggin I up - goen it im Dave!

Dohnee
Doesn't he
Ah, ee looks evsa sad dohnee.

Dollop
A lump of something
I'll jus have a dollop of mash.

Done
Did
Ee done that yeserday.

Down
To
Weem goen down ar muh's later.

Dowtown
Broadmead or The City Centre
Comen dowtown?

Drawlen
An illustration
I done this drawlen at school fer ar muh.

Dreckly
Straight away
I went dreckly ohm.

Drive
A bus/taxi driver
Next stop drive/Cheers drive.

Drived

Drove
I drived ar muh down Asdawl smornen.

Dunny

Doesn't he
Ee looks jus like is muh dunny.

Dunt

Don't/Doesn't
Ar muh dunt like they cakes mind.

Dursn't

Dare not
I dursn't tell ar ole man what I dun to is gawf clubs.

Eadfit
To lose your temper
Ee ad a right eadfit when ee sawl I broke it.

Eda
He does
Eda really luv that Fiestawl mind.

Eddlice
Headlights
Yer, yoom gone an left your eddlice on.

Ee
He/Him/This/That/It
Ee's a right nutjob ee is/Me ammer? Ee's over there.

Eem
He/It is
Eem gonna tell Ar Ole Man I bin smoken weed.

Ee's A Bed
He is in bed
Ar Ole Man? Ee's a bed.

Eeuz
He was
Ee cudda told I eeuz goen out.

Eeve
He has
Eeve only told Ar Muh I was up the Gas mind!

El Dub

An area of North West Bristol; Lawrence Weston (see Larnce Wesson)
El Dub? Iss down past Wessbree, by Shire.

Elemm

Eleven
Ee only looks bout elemm but they still served ee.

Embray

An area of West Bristol; Henbury
Embray? Thas up by Blaze innum.

Engrove

An area of South Bristol; Hengrove
Oi, snot bleeden Nawl Wess! Iss Engrove!

Enlees

An area of West Bristol; Henleaze
Iss proper posh up Enlees, but taint no Cliffun mind.

Eppy

Fit of madness/Headfit
She ad a right eppy when I tawd er.

Er

Or
Oozee mean, ee er I?

Erd

Heard
I erd your muh's a nutter.

Err

Her
I told err no already.

Evsa

Ever so
Ee's evsa ansum I reckon. Proper lush.

Evun

Heaven
Fer evuns sake!

Eyar

Here you are
Swannit do ee? Eyar then.

Falled

To fall
I falled down an ole yeserday, scraged me ass.

Famlay

Family
Is famlay is all gleeners mind.

Fanks

Thank you
Is that un fer me? Fanks!

Fansay

Fancy
They cakes looks a bit fansay!

Fatchers

A popular West Country cider; Thatchers
Ar Ole Man don't know I. Taint dementia mind, ees been on the Fatchers.

Fawder

Folder
Ida keep all photawls from me olidays in that fawder.

Feeder

The Feeder Canal
I got this bike out the Feeder, but eem proper smart.

Fer
For
Gif I it yer, I'll do it fer ee.

Feud
If you had
Fued ad the day I've ad...

Fick
Thick
Ee's a fick as two short planks ee is.

Fiestawl
Ford Fiesta
Ee got a Fiestawl XR2i. Eem a proper boy racer.

Fill-Un
An area of North Bristol; Filton
They made that concord up Fill-Un.

Fin
Thin
Ee's a smart diet, sheem as fin as ell.

Fine
Find
Jew fine your phone yeserday?

Fink
Think
I bin finken about goen down Carboot Circus. Comen?

Fire Up
To beat up
You better go, ee wants to fire you up.

Florawl

A popular vegetable oil spread
Swant florawl on ee luv?

Ford

Forward or Afford
I look ford to it/I casn't ford it this munf.

Forn

A popular alcoholic apple drink; Blackthorn
Anudder Forn in yer fry Darlen.

Fornbree

A small town north of Bristol; Thornbury
I got ee of a bloke in Fornbree.

Fotawl

Photograph
Sheda ave a lush fotawl of the baby from the osbidal. Taint even born yet

Fought

Thought
I fought you said ee was lush?

Fowstay

Disgusting/Mouldy
I ain't eaten that it's all fowstay.

Fowzand

Thousand
It only cost I free fowzand pown.

Frages
For ages
Aint seen ee round yer frages. As ee?

Frampun Cotral
Frampton Cotterell; A small village north east of Bristol
No this ain't bleeden Yate! Iss Frampun Cotral!

Free
Three
Free lamps? Eeem be up Taardown me babber.

Frim
For him
Hey! They chips is frim.

Frizz
For his
Whas ee want frizz birfday?

Froat
Throat
Ee ad 'Cut here' tattooed cross is froat; looks gurt mint.

Frontline
An infamous area of St Paul's; Grosvenor Road
Get they off a bloke down the Frontline?

Fru

Through
They razbrizz went right fru I!

Fruneral

Funeral
Jew see that fruneral? Ee was luverly.

Fry

For I/me
Awd dis un fry ullee.

Fur-err

For her
Ee said it was jus fur-err mind.

Furrplay

A personal congratulations; Fair play
Thas yourn? Furrplay to you mate!

Furzday

Thursday
Ar ole man down the job centre on a Furzday. Ee's only looking mind.

Gate, The

Home of Bristol City Football Club; Ashton Gate
Bin down Gate Geoff – weem rubbish.

Gas, The

Bristol Rovers Football Club
Gas is going up, mind!

Gashead

A supporter of Bristol Rovers football club
They'm all Gasheads down Banjo Island.

Gawf

Golf
Taint proper Gawf wivout a wimmill mind.

Gawld

Gold
I got free quid for me filling up Cash for Gawd.

Gay

Sad/Uncool
Them trainers is so gay!

Gibbim

Gave him/Give him
Jew gibbim your phone number?

Gif I it

Give that to me
Oi! Gif I it yer.

Ginormous

Smaller than gigantic but bigger
than enormous
They petezawls is ginormous!

Giss

Give me
Yer, giss one a they ullee?

Glenner

A person who is a couple
of toppers short of a full
loaf (Derived from Glenside
Psychiatric Hospital) (derog.)
Ee's a right glenner mind!

Glider

An alcoholic drink of fermented
apples; Cider
*Ee ad like twenny pints a glider up
the Corrie Tap!*

Goa

Go to
I gotta goa bed now.

Gob/Gobbed

Spit/Spat
That basdurd jus gobbed on I!

Goes

Going
I goes on me olides next week.

Golnill

Golden Hill, an area of North West Bristol
They still built that Tesco up Golnill mind!

Gonna

Going to
Ee's gonna get it when I gets awld of ee.

Gotta

Got to
Yoom gotta eat your greens or yawl get scurvy.

Grampfer

Grandfather
Ar Grampfer lost is marbles. Finks eem Donna Summer!

Grampfer Grey

Woodlouse
Jew see 'That Grampher Grey's Got Talent' on ITV. Loada bleeden rubbish.

Granner

Grandmother
You stayen wiv I or goen with your Granner?

Guddun
A good one
Ee's ell of a guddun ee is.

Guff/Guffed
To break wind
Blige! Ast thee guffed?

Gurls
Girls
Wonna chat some gurls up? They all luvs I.

Gurt Biggun
SS Great Britain
Wernit dat bloke wiv the macky at that made the SS Gurt Biggun?

Gurt/Gert
Very
Er ands is gurt macky. Sure taint a bloke?

Gwahn
Go on
Ah gwahn, please.

Gwahn En
Go on then
Goen? Gwahn en. Ee won't be mist by I.

This section has been left intentionally blank as no Bristolian ever pronounces the letter 'H' at the start of a word.

I
I have or Me
I bin out all day wiv Ar Muh/That belongs to I.

Ideawl
An idea
I got an ideawl, get that un.

Ijut
Idiot
Ee's a bleeden ijut ee is!

Ikeawl
A large popular Swedish furniture store; Ikea
Ee works down Ikeawl on a Furzday.

Ill
Hill
I got forty out me fiestawl going down ill.

Im
Him
Don't tell I, tell im!

Inchew
Aren't you
Inchew cold in dat yungun?

Innit
Isn't it
Thas Ar Muh's dress innit Dave?

Innum   Isn't it/he/she or Aren't they
Ark at they, they'm full a crap innum.

Int   Is/Am Not
*Ee's a bad un int ee/I int goen
dowtown.*

Ippadroam   Bristol Hippodrome
*They got Cinderellawl on down
Ippodrom mind.*

Is   His
Oi! Dats is dinner notchores!

Ise   I am
Ise goen a Severn Beach for me olides.

Iself   Himself
*Ee fitted that gas boiler iself. Ee don't
know nuffink bout plumbin mind.*

Iss   It is
Snot mine! Iss ar Dave's.

Itchy-barry   Bristolian derivative of 'itchy-chin'.
Declaration of disbelief
*Yoom friends wiv Bob Crampton on
Facebook? Dats a Itchy Barry!*

Jamicawl

An island in the West Indies
Jamicawl Street's snot in Jamicawl mind!

Jammer

Somebody who is very lucky
Ee won a tenner on the lottery. Ee's a right jammer.

Jammy

Lucky
Ee's only gone and won the meat raffle again the jammy bleeder.

Jan

Tramp (derog.)
Jew get that coat out the bin? You steppy jan!

Jasper

Wasp
I got stung by a jasper on me Fatchers awdin and!

Jeerme

Did you hear me?
You ain't goen out atawl now, jeerme?

Jew

Do/Did you
Jew fink sheda kiss I?

Jigsawl

Jigsaw
Ee aint upside down, iss a jigsawl of Australial!

Jitter

A person with long hair (derog.)
Get thee aircut or yoom look like a jitter.

Kangsood
A town north east of Bristol;
Kingswood
*Chasers? What up Kangswood? Nah,
I don't wanna ave a fight tonight.*

Keener
Somebody who works hard
(derog.)
*Ee done all his ohmwerk, ee's a right
keener.*

Kerbab
Traditional Turkish fayre; Doner
Kebab
*Whas ee want on this kerbab then
me babber?*

Kiddie
Boy/Youth (anything up to mid-
twenties)
What im? Ee's just a kiddie.

Kinave
Can I Have
Canave one a they?

Koffay
Coffee
*Greggs do's koffay but's evsa
spensive mind.*

Lackey Band
Elastic Band
Ee flicked I wiv a lackey band.

Laff
Laugh
Made I laff.

Lamminutt
Laminate
I got em to lamiminutt me fotawl of Caffy Barry.

Largurr
Lager beer
Dis Harp largurr tastes like piss.

Larnce Wesson
An area of North West Bristol; Lawrence Weston (see El Dub)
Long Cross? Yeah, eem down Larnce Wesson innum.

Laters
See you later
Yoom off? OK, laters.

Lav
I will have
Ullee get off that phone or lav a gurt macky bill.

Lease
Least
At lease I dint say nuffink!

Lectric

Electric
*Eel need a gurt long stension lead
wiv one a they lectric cars, mind!*

Led

To lie down (past tense)
I bin led down all day.

Leebim/Leebem

Leave him/them
Leebim to it.

Leevellen

Evening
Jew get the leevellen post?

Lemerlade/Lemnade

Lemonade
*Ar Muh brung I some lemerlade and
it were lush.*

Lend

Borrow
Jew fink ill lend I is skelington outfit?

Lent

Borrowed
*I lent ee out from the Liebree; aint
taking it back mind!*

Les

Let us
*Les pray; Ar Ole Man, who art in
eaven…..*

Lessaf
Can I have
Lessaf a go on yer tractor!

Lesson
Less than
I got lesson I fought I was gonna get for Ar Mah's gawld!

Lidawz
German budget supermarket chain; Lidl
She works down Lidawz now mind.

Liebree
Library
Sno thee aint allowed to tawk up the liebree mind.

Like
See Pronunciation Guide

Lissen
Listen
Jus lissen to ee, ee finks ee da know it all.

Lit Lun
A young child
Thee casn't even smack a lit lun no more.

Look
See Pronunciation Guide

Lower Cliffun   Estate agent jargon for the area
of Southville, South Bristol
*Ee got a luverly flat down Lower
Cliffun way mind – cheap anhall.*

Lush   Very nice
*Eda fink eem proper lush, but ee
ain't.*

Luverly   Lovely
*Sheda ave a luverly bunch of
coconuts mind.*

Luvver   Friend/Mate (non sexual)
Alright me Luvver?

A-Z

Macky　　　　　　Very big
Look at the gurt macky hooter on ee!
Tis like Concord!

Marnen　　　　　　Morning
Gotta pick ar Muh up in marnen.

Masarge　　　　　　Massage
Taint that sorta masarge mind.

Maul, The　　　　　A large shopping centre at Cribbs
Causeway; The Mall
Evsa spensive out the Maul mind.

Mauve Yer　　　　　I'm over here
Where am I? Mauve yer look.

Mawday　　　　　　Mouldy
They cakes is aw bleeden mawday!

Mazen　　　　　　Amazing
No way! Thas bleeden mazen!

Me　　　　　　　My
Me head's killen I.

Meader　　　　　　A resident of Southmead (derog.)
Shaint goen out wiv a Meader is she?

Mem, The

The Memorial Stadium
Bin up the Mem Geoff – weem rubbish!

Member

To remember
Member that bird you pulled up Chasers? Wot a munter!

Mentalist

To be mental/mad/psychologically disturbed
Ee's a bit of a mentalist mind!

Meryl

Mayor
Weem got one a they proper Meryl's now, but eda wear funny trousers mind.

Meself

Myself
Might as well do it meself.

Miat

My hat
Yoom sat on miat you spanner.

Mied

My head
Mied's gone.

Mind

See Pronunciation Guide

Mint   Very good
Thas mint! Cheers!

Moron   More than
Ee aint got moron I ave ee?

Muh   Mother
Ar Muh's down the Bingo gain.

Munf   Month
*Shaint gonna go out wiv ee in a munf
of Furzdays!*

Mungry   I am hungry
Muh mungry, whas fer tea?

Munt   Not very nice
I ain't eaten they! They cakes munt!

Munter   A person who's not very attractive
(derog.)
*Your Muh aint no Milf sheem a
munter*

Murr   Mirror
*Murr Murr on the wall, whose gurt
lush like?*

Nawl Wess

An area of South Bristol; Knowle West
They tawlks proper Bristle up Nawl Wess Mind

Nebbersin

Never seen
I aint nubbersin nuffink like it.

Needawz

Needles
I got pinz an needawz agenn!

Needs

Require
Yoom needs a bath, yoom stink.

Neever

Neither
Ee dint see I neever.

Neffam

A steep hill leading to the Feeder Canal; Netham
I bin fishen down the Neffam. Never got nuffink mind.

Nellzee

A town west of Bristol; Nailsea
They got letric down Nellzee now mind.

Nerr

Never
You dint win? Nerr mind.

No

Not
Fancy goen out wiv I then or no?

Notchores

Not yours
If it's notchores, whose it belong too?

Nowse

Knows
Ar Ole Man nowse that Bob Crampton; taint an itchy barry tis true!

Nuffink

Nothing
Eel get nuffink out of I.

Nuh Night

Goodnight
Nuh night darlen, I'll see thee tamorra.

Nurlay

Nearly
Jew see I nurlay go a pisser?

Of Have
I could of brung it home but I dint.

Off Of Off
Where do ee get off of a bus en?

Oh Ah I understand/Oh yes
Oh ah, I knows ee.

Ohm Home
I bin sat ohm all day.

Olides Holidays
Ee bin on is olides.

Ondawl Honda
Ee got one a they smart Ondawl Civics.

Oo Who
Right, oo called I a bleeden munter?

Oops Hoop style earings
Is they your bird's gawd oops?

Ooze Who is
There ain't nobody ooze fer the war ere.

Oozee

Who does he
Oozee know down ere?

Oozeefink

Who does he think
Oozeefink ee is?

Ore Field

An area of North Bristol; Horfield
Ar ole mans in Ore Field.

Orse

An animal for riding, not eating;
Horse
Yer, they burgers got orse innum?

Osbidal

Hospital
*I bin up the osbidal wiv ar muh all
night.*

Ow

How or Out
*Ow'd ee do dat?/Look ow, ansum,
yer she comes.*

Ow Bist?

How are you?
Awlrite? Ow bist?

Pacifically Specifically
Ee pacifically said to put it yer.

Painen Giving pain/To be in pain
*I gotta see a dentist, me tuff's painen
I rotten.*

Pardunn/Parn Pardon
Pardunn I

Parler Tawk Former Bristolian hip-hop crew;
Parlour Talk
*Erd that Padlocked Tonic? Them
Parler Tawk blokes is mint.*

Pataytawls Potatoes
*Ee's growing some gurt macky
pataytawls down is allockments*

Peepaw People
*Dohnnee know how many peepaw is
coming to is party?*

Pennety Penalty
*They shitheads got a pennety in the
las minute the jammy bleeders.*

Petezawlut
A popular pizza restaurant; Pizza Hut
Petezawlet? Ar ole man wont eat none of that foreign muck.

Petrawl
Petrol
Eda get is petrawl down Asdawl mind.

Pewjoe
A French car manufacturer
Blige, jew see that Pewjoe? Ee was lush!

Picka
Pickle
Ise going ave picka on my ploughmans. Gurt lush!

Pigsty III
An area of Gloucester Rd known only by residents and bus drivers.
Ore Field Prison? Yeah, thas up by Pigsty III.

Pirates, The
Bristol Rovers Football Club
Whas wanna sport they Pirates for? Theys a loada bleeden rubbish!

Pitchen
Settling Snow
Tis snowen out, but snot pitchen mind.

Pitcher Picture
Err face were a proper pitcher

Plasterscene Plasticine
They makes them Wallace and Gromit outta plasterscence dunnum

Plenny Plenty
Sheda get plenny a action mind for a munter

Polski Sklep Local shop selling delicacies all named with the letters Z and K.
Jew get they Kaszanka down a Polski Sklep?

Por'ersed Portishead, a coastal town near Bristol
We went swimmen down Por'sersed; got diarrheaul mind.

Pot Nuda Pot Noodle
Ar Muh did us Turkay Pot Nuda for our Crizmuz dinner

Pown Pound
If I ad a pown for every time ee said that…

Praps Perhaps
Praps sheda ave the ump wiv you

Prawln Cocktell Prawn Cocktail
Smatter wiv that Prawln Cocktell? I'll finish ee!

Prittee Pretty
Shaint prittee; shem a right munter

Proper Excellent
They clothes from George at Asdawl be proper smart

Proper Job A job well done
Ee done a proper job painten that car wiv Dulux. Proper smart ee looks now.

Puddies Hands
Blige! Me puddies is bleeden cawd!

Putnin Put it in
Jew putnin in the paper for I?

Puwher Computer
Ar yungun knows ow to work the puwher mind, dunt he?

Pyeanhalf

A pint and a half
*Canave a pyeanhalf of Fatchers
please me luvver.*

Pyjarmers

Pyjamas
*She got I they pyjarmers down
Ranjanis. Snot allowed near the fire
in em mind!*

Quicken

A fast one
Blige! Ee's a quicken innum!

Quipmant

Equipment
*Ee got all the proper quipmant fer
doen the job mind.*

Raggy   Hand rolled cigarette
                 Swanna raggy?

Rawl   A bread roll
                 They am rawls looks lush!

Razbrizz   Raspberries
                 They got razbrizz in them mind.

Replicawl   A copy; Replica
                 Don't buy ee, iss jus a replicawl.

Rit   Wrote
                 I rit to ar dad in Ore Field smornen.

Robins, The Bristol City Football Club
                 The Robins is goen up!

Rown   Around
                 You dint walk rown town like that?

Rowna   Around the
                 Ee keeps is car rowna back mind!

Rus   Or else
                 Gif I it yer rus I'll belt thee!

Sabout   It's about
Sabout time ee got iself a job innit

Sadly Broke   A housing development North of
Bristol; Bradley Stoke
*They got shops up Sadly Broke now
annall mind*

Safternun   This afternoon
*I ain't goen back a work safternun
mind.*

Saint   This/That is not
Yer Dave, saint rite is it?

Salid   Salad
Saild in me Kebabs all mawday

Saul   It is all
Saul a loada crap if eda ask I.

Saunawl   Sauna
*Ar Muh's front room's like a bleeden
saunawl*

Sawd   Sold
Tis sawd as seen mind!

Sawl

Saw
I sawl is ole man up Asdal

Scaw

School
*Weem up that scaw every five
minutes wiv ee*

Scowen

Are you going
Scowen up Chasers wiv I?

Scrage

To graze/scratch yourself
I fell over an scraged me knee.

Scrumps

Small pieces of fried batter
*Yoom not get fin eating Scurmps
mind.*

Scud

A scab (as result of a scrage)
I got a macky scud on me knee.

Scummy

Not very nice/Dirty
*They toilets down Vassels are bleein
scummy*

Scutler

A promiscuous girl (derog.)
Shaint a scutler is she?

Scutlers

Lambert and Butler cigarettes
Ee's on twenny Scutlers a day; ee's only ten mind.

See

See Pronunciation Guide

Seegaw

Seagull
They seegawls loves scrumps dunt they?

Seen

Saw
I seen er up the cinemawl

Seenin

Saw him
Las time I seenin ee were up Chasers.

Semm

Seven
I reckon the Gas is gonna score semm safternoon

Sex Ample

To set an example
Ee better sex ample to they lit luns mind!

Shag

A friend/mate
Awlrite shag!

Shaint

She isn't
Shaint right in the ead; sheem shot away!

Sheda

She does
Sheda love Ar Ole Man dunt she?

Shire

An area of West Bristol; Shirehampton (see Shrampton)
Much nicer down Shire than down El Dub mind.

Shithead

A fan of Bristol City football club (derog.)
Me own muh's a shithead! I don't wanna believe it!

Shoo-en

A beating
Sheda giv im a right shooen when she been on the zider

Shot Away

Mad/Insane
Twenny quid fer that? You gotta be shot away.

Shrammed

To feel really cold
Shut them bleeden doors, I's shrammed in yer!

Shrampton
An area of West Bristol; Shirehampton (see Shire)
Ar nan lives down off Shrampton Green. Sheda get the 40 ohm.

Shup
Shut up
Dunny ever shup bout it?

Simler
Similar
Ee's simler to that un I got.

Sint
Saint/St.
Jew see that Sint Christoper round is neck; proper smart like.

Skelington
Skeleton
Thees better watch that Weight Watchers mind or yawl end up like a skelington

Skooze
Excuse me
Skooze I, pardon I, beers comen frew.

Skunna
It is going to
Skunna piss down later mind!

Sleever

A straight pint glass
Stick that forn in a sleever darlen - iss fer the missus.

Slider

Children's playground slide
Eda go up the slider the wrong way

Smart

Very nice
They clothes at Matalan is proper smart

Smatter

What is the matter?
Smatter wiv Ar Ole Man? Ee wont tawk to I!

Smoothen the cat

Stroking the cat
Ee ad an asthamaul attack after smoothen the cat

Smornen

This morning
Bus took frages to come smornen

Snell

Small slimy creature eaten by the French.
Taint only orses they eat in France mind; they'da love their snells annall.

Sno

Do you know
Sno when ees comen?

Snot

It is not
Snot mine, tis is!

Souf Americawl

The continent of South America
Yer, City got a yungun from Souf Americawl

Soufmeed

Southmead, an area of North Bristol
She visited I out Soufmeed Osbidal

Spanner

An idiot
Dats the wrong spanner you spanner

Spawnay

Lucky
Yoom nuffink but a spawnay git.

Spect so

I expect so
Muh, can I ave petezawl fer me tee? Spect so.

Spenshun

Suspension
I gave er a lift ome from Weight Watchers, like, and she nearly broke me spenshun

Spensive

Expensive
Eee got I some sepnsive choclut for me birfday

Speshly

Especially
I made it speshly for you me babber.

Spike Island

A collective of art studios and workshops sited in a former Brooke Bond tea factory near the Floating Harbour
Jew see they drawlens down Spike Island? Proper smart.

Spinner

Liar
They ain't yours you bleeden spinner!

Spit

It is a bit
Spit late to tell I now!

Spooner

Somebody who is not very bright (derog.)
Ow did ee manage to put is cacks over is trousers the spooner!

Spoony

Uncool
They daps is a bit spoony

Spose

I suppose
Spose I gotta ave a go now anneye.

Spreethed

Rough cracked skin through cold
It wunaff cawd! Ar ands got all spreethed.

Stayshun

Station
We was waiting frages for a train at Warmley stayshun, wasn't us?

Steller

A popular lager beer; Stella Artois
Hoffmiester's off! Thee fansy a Steller?

Stingers

Stinging Nettles
Wudjew get the ball out the stingers for I?

Summut

Something
Snot safe to cross ere there's summat comen

Sumpfen

Something
Jew don't get sumpfen for nuffink.

Sunner

A male friend/mate (non sexual)
Awlrite me ole sunner, ow bist?

Swannee

Do you want this? (usually asked when brandishing a fist or weapon. A threat)
Swannee er wot?

Swant/Swanna

Do you want?
Swanna dance the funky chicken wiv I?

Swellead

An arrogant smug self satisfied person
Oooh ark at ee, gurt swellead.

Swemmen

Swimming
Only rats goes swemmen down the docks mind?

Swot

It is what
Swot I always wanted!

Syew

It is you
Tis innit? Syew! I fought so.

Ta
To
Tell I when wedda get ta where ee is.

Taardown
An area of South Bristol; Totterdown
Free lamps, thas up Taardown.

Taint
It isn't
Taint alf ot muh.

Tamorra
Tomorrow
Snot today, tis tamorra

Tawd
Told
I tawd err straight, I bleeden ates you I said.

Tawk
Talk
Whas wanna tawk to ee for?

Thas
That is
That the way to do it, like.

That Ain't Right
Is that correct?
I erd you got the sack, that ain't right?

The Kiddies
The best
They'm the kiddies alright!

A-Z

Thee
You
Whas wrong with thee?

Them
Those
Them were the days

Theys/They'm
They are
They'm on bout putting a man on Mars; planet mind, not the choclut bar

Thur
There
Are we thur yet? Are we thur yet? Are we thur yet? Ullee bleeden shup!!

Thuther/Tuther
The other
I turnt tother cheek before I ead butted im

Tight
Mean
Ee's tight as a Badger's arse!

Tis
It is
Thas notchores! Tis. Taint. Tis. Whatever.

Tisunt
It is not
Iss tonight innit? Tisunt! Snot till tomorrow!"

To

Used as a reference to a location.
Wheres that to? Where you to?

Toon

To him
I said toon, ee casn't ave it!

Topper

The end piece of a loaf of bread
Giv I the topper for me lunch

Trimmens

Christmas decorations
I gotta get the trimmens down from the loft.

Tuff

Tooth
What time do the tuff fairy get here Muh?

Tuffbrush

Toothbrush
I got a new tuffbrush down Asdawl today.

Tump

A small grassy Hill
Watch I rawl down this tump.

Tunawl

A large tasty fish in a can
Tell Ar Muh to get I a tunawl rawl from Greggs

Turbo Island

A small patch of Stokes Croft grass frequented by cider-drinking street folk.
They likes their zider up Turbo Island mind!

Turkay

Turkey
They turkay twizzlers are mazen

Turnt

Turned
You shoulda turnt left not right.

Twas

It was
That wasn't yourn! Twas you glenner!

Twasnt/Twant

It was not
Twasn't I, twas im!

Twat

To hit
Ee was dogging Ar Ole man up so I twatted im

Twenny

Twenty
Twenny Scutlers please me babber

Twot

Too hot
Africal's twot for I!

A-Z

Uddent / Unt / Ussent
Wouldn't
I uddent mess wiv ee mind. Ee's ard!

Ulbum
A collection of musical tracks on one disc
You erd that new Por'ersed ulbum? Iss mint!

Ullee
Will you
Jus bleedin shut up ullee!

Un
One
I got gurt big un.

Ungray
Hungry
Is ee ungray? Swant some tea?

Up
To
Jus goen up the shops Muh awlrite?

Up The Downs
Going to/On Durdham Downs
I ad err up the downs.

Urrlay
Early
I aint getten up that urrlay mind!

Urt
Pain
Bleenell that urts!

Vawlse

Vase
Jus stick they flowers in that vawlse fry ullee.

Vegabull

Vegatable
Do ee ave vegabulls with petezawl?

Vench

Adventure playground; notably Lockleaze
Comen up the vench?

Verrewkawl

Verruca
Thee casn't goa swimen baffs wiv a verrewkawl.

Vidjoe

Video
Jew set the vidjoe fer Shoestring?

Virrickawl

Vehicle
I drives a public service virrickawl.

Volly, The

A public house on King Street; *The Naval Volunteer*
Wanna pint down the Volly?

A - Z

Wackum

To hit somebody
Cas ee wackum fry? Ee called ar muh a munter.

Wall

Wool
Muh, got any cotton wall?

Wallop

A hit
Ar ole man's gonna give I a right wallop later.

Wanna

Want to
Wanna go down a Beat 'em an Wackum?

Warter

Water
Muh, canave some warter?

Was

Were
We was over there. Now weem yer.

Wassat

What was that
Yer, wassat noise?

Wasson

What is on
Wasson the tele muh?

Wayten

Waiting
I cassant keep wayten frim all me life.

Weeda

We do
Thas not what weeda need ere.

Weem

We are
Weem in a right mess now Stanley.

Wells

Wales, a country close to Bristol
I bin over Wells watchen that Tom Jones.

Went A Pisser

To fall badly
Ar Clive's muh tripped up the stairs and went a pisser.

Were

Was
Ee were full of crap.

Werk

Work
I bin a werk safternun anneye. Stacken stuff down Asdawl.

Wernit

Wasn't it
Top do las night wernit!

Werse/Wheres   Where have/did you
Werse get ee to?

Wessbree   An area of North West Bristol;
Westbury-on-Trym
*Snot Soufmeed! Iss bleeden
Wessbree!*

Wesson   A coastal resort on the Bristol
Channel; Weston-super-Mare
Ee travelled up from Wesson to see I

Wester   A resident of Knowle West
(derog.)
Is muh's a proper wester mind.

Weverspoons   Popular chain of public houses; J
D Wetherspoons
*Yer, I sawl ar muh up Weverspoons
wiv your ole man las night!*

Whas   What are/do (you) or What is
*Whas up to?/Whas fink?/Whas up
wiv ee?*

Whas Ee Chatbout?   What is he talking about?
*That Stephen Hawking – whas ee
chatbout?*

Whas Fink?
What do you think
Whas fink of ee then me babber? A beauty innum.

Whas Mean?
What do you mean
Whas mean ee dunt wonna go?

Whas Want?
What do you want?
Whas want me to do bout it? Aint my fault ee assant got no clean cacks.

Whasser
What is the
Whasser bleeden point? Nuffink aint gonna appen.

Where Weetoo?
Where are we?
Where weetoo now Muh?

Where You To/ Where Bis?
Where are you?
I casn't find ee, where you to?

Wheres
Where have/did you
Wheres get ee to?

Wheres Attoo?
Where is that?
Baff? Wheres attoo?

Wheres Bin?

Where have you been?
Wheres bin aw me life?

Wheres Eetoo?

Where is he?
I knows ee's yer the basdurd! Wheres eetoo?

Wheres Gettee?

Where did you get that?
Wow, proper smart fotawl a concord, wheres gettee to?

Wheres Goen?

Where are you going?
Wheres goen to me babber?

Widdywud

An area of South Bristol; Withywood
Yer drive, is this un goen up Widdywud?

Widjew

With you
You bring that game widjew?

Will

Wheel
Jew sells wills?

Will Barrel

Wheelbarrow
I done me gardnen wiv a will barrel.

Wimmilill	An area of South Bristol; Windmill Hill *Whas mean there aint no wimmill up Wimmilill?*
Windawl	Window *Yer, open them windawls will ee?*
Wiv	With *Whas avin wiv your chips? Scrumps?*
Wobby	What are you *Wobby on about?*
Wonna	Want to *Wonna go dowtown wiv I? Ar muhs goen.*
Wudjew	Would you *Wudjew go out with me mate? Eda fink yoom proper lush.*
Wunaff	Wasn't half *Ee wunaff good looken!*
Wunt	Was not *I wunt even gonna do that!*

Xterr A city in Devon; Exeter
I went from Parkway down to Xterr.

Yawl

You will
Yawl ave me bleeden fist if thee ain't bleeden quiet.

Yeerin

Hearing
Ee needs is bleeden yerrin testen.

Yer

Hey/Excuse me or Here or Ear (singular)
Yer you seen ar little un? Yeah ee's over yer.

Yer Awl

Earhole
Ow many studs you got in that yer awl?

Yer Tis

Here it is
Ave ee seen me special fotawl of ar muh? Yeah, yer tis.

Yerrens

Earings
Thems nice yerrings, is they gawld?

Yers

Ears
Sabout time you cleant yers out.

Yeserday
Yesterday
I went dowtown yeserday, I ain't goen safternun annall.

Yewar
Here you are
Yewar ave this un ee's better.

Yewman
Human
Jew see that Bein Yewman? First uns was filmed in Taardown.

Yoom
You are/have
Yoom right clever you is/Yoom left your wallet ohm?

Yourn
Yours
Zat yourn?

Yuey
UWE (University of the West of England), a former polytechnic on the outskirts of the city
Oh, yoom only at the yuey.

Yungun
Somebody younger than yourself
They yunguns bin in yer again tryen a buy Fatchers!

Zackley   Exactly
Thas zackly ow I dun it!

Zat   Is that
Zat un youn?

Zider   An alcoholic drink of fermented
apples; Cider
Zider I right up ar kid!

Useful Phrases

Listen to him boasting on about his trip to the States!
Ark at ee chatting on bout Americawl, the bleeden swellead!

We have spent a spiffing day at the coast sampling the local delicacies
We ad chips and a bag of doughnuts down Wesson!

We are not flying from the Midlands; we are flying from Bristol International Airport.
Snot Burmenan, tis Lulsgate we be flying from

My mother has brought me home an unusual gift from her holidays
Ar Muh got I a shrunken ead from Africawl. Taint pritee mind!

They have some unusual customs across the Bridge
They'm all sheep shaggers in Wells mind!

Did you visit the Great Wall of China whilst on your holidays?
Yer, jew see the Gurt Macky wall of Chinawl?

Why is it there is no driver for this vehicle?
Wheres a bleeden driver to?

I wish to leave your vehicle at the next available authorised stopping point please.
Next stop drive.

I say, where exactly are we?
Where we to?

Excuse me young sir, you appear to be getting into my taxi.
Yer yongun, dees better get out a there or diesel gettee.

By Jove, you appear to have placed your motor vehicle into such a position that reversing it may prove to be problematic.
Yer, thee's got'n where thee casn't back'n hassen't?

I'm sorry to have to tell you children, but the upper floor of this vehicle is non-smoking.
Oi! Put they bleeden fags out or I'll tell thee ole man.

Would this service take me to the city centre?
Do this un go dowtown?

Excuse me driver, could you possibly provide me with change from a twenty-pound note?
Yer drive, cas ee change this un fry?

This service appears to running extremely late.
Blige, wheres bin?

I am slightly concerned about the beef content in your Lasagne
Yer, taint full of orse is it?

I wish to purchase items for a family picnic
Gis I four cans of Fatchers, a sausage rawl and a bag of monster munch.

I am not sure this plate of Corden Bleu food will provide me with enough sustenance
Yer Waiter, kinave a dollop of mash wiv ee?

The edge has been taken off my al fresco dining experience
Blige, a gurt Macky Seagawl just dumped in me monster munch!

If you are not careful your dietary habits may lead to obesity
Yer, yoom wonna cut down on your pork life mate and get some exercise

I believe I have over indulged on my first visit to Za Za Bazaar and may require urgent medical attention
Ullee take I down a ospidal to ave me stomach pumped

What accompaniments would you like with your traditional Turkish fayre?.
Whas want on this Kerbab?

The Indian food appears to have unsettled my father's stomach
Ar Ole man's at ome with diarrheawl - Ar Muh's ad a open the windawls cause it bleeden stinks

Proprietor, I wish to purchase a pint of reassuringly expensive Belgian lager.
Pint a Steller me ole babber.

Please can you furnish me with your wine list?
Zider I up lanlord.

Barmaid, please could I have one more.
Gif I anudder un in yer darlen.

Please can you pass on my compliments to the chef as my meal was outstanding.
Yer mate, that was gurt lush!

Can you direct me to the local patisserie?
Wheres Greggs to?

I say, that tuna baguette does appear awfully large.
Blige, dat tunawl rawls gurt macky.

Would it be possible to sample a selection of your delicate pastries?
Gis I a steak bake anna sausage rawl me luvver.

Excuse me, I think you will find there is a mistake in this bill.
Yer, yooms tryen to rob I blind you basdurd!

Do you think I could have a rather large portion of potato?
Gif I a gurt macky dollop of ee ullee?

Can you tell me, is there a traditional Italian restaurant close to here?
Wheres there a petezawlut rown yer?

I am a bit hesitant about my prostate examination and where you are planning to place that expensive piece of medical equipment
Ee finks ee's shoving dat camrawl where the sun dunt shine ee got anudder fink coming

He has gone to seek urgent medical attention following a disagreement in a local hostelry
Ee's in Soufmeed Osbidal after ee got a shoo-en down the local

I do not think your condition is influenza but is in fact an upper respiratory tract infection
Snot flu tis a cawd

I am not sure I understand your medical diagnosis
Whas ee chatbout?

I think this person is deceased but I need a second opinion
I fink ee's a dedun; whas fink?

Excuse me Doctor, I believe my mother is suffering from psychiatric problems.
Yer Doc, ar Muh's shot away.

My father is suffering chest pains and may require urgent medical attention.
Get ar ole man to the ospidal, ee's aven an arrtack.

I have a vaginal infection, please can you inform my family.
I got an itchy box, cas ee call ar muh fry.

I have been feeling rather unwell and I believe my bowels may be loose.
I fink I got diarrheawl.

I'm sorry, you must be mistaken, I simply cannot be pregnant.
Shut up! I dint even do it wiv im!

I have had a toothache for some time now.
Me tuff's been painen I frages.

Following an altercation with my sibling, I believe I may have injured my testicles.
Ar bruvver jus kicked I in me baws!

I appear to be suffering difficulty breathing and require medicine to correct it.
I got asthmawl, gif I a puff on ee.

I am suffering greatly from pain due to inflamation.
Bleenell, iss gurt macky!

The lively discussion concerning taxi queue etiquette ended rather abruptly.
I fink me jaws discolated.

Excuse me kind sir, I believe my sight to be failing me.
Yer, I casn't see a bleeden fing. Not nuffink mind!

She appears to have lost an awful amount of weight, are you sure she is not suffering from anorexia?
Blige, sheda look like a right bleeden skelington!

I say, can you see the large stomach on that gentleman?
Look at the gurt macky gut on ee!

Please help me, my mother fell from a great height.
Yer, ar muh went a pisser down the stairs.

Could you please call me an ambulance?
Cas ee get an amblance fry?

Phrases

Excuse me young man but you appear to be looking at me in a threatening manner.
Yer, yungun, you dogging I up?

He had a brief conversation with the door supervisor regarding nightclub etiquette
The bouncer twatted im!

Kingswood's finest night spot will be frequented by more mature ladies this evening
Iss grab a granny up Chasers tonight mind

We enjoyed a traditional Bavarian evening with a Bristolian twist
We went down the Bierkeller for some steins of Fatchers and a scrap wiv the welsh

I'm afraid your attire does not meet the club's strict dress policy
Yoom not coming in ere wiv daps on

You just have to see the spectacular stage show at the gentleman's club
Fansay coming to the strip club to see some scutlers dancing in their cacks

Hello Miss. Whilst I don't think your friend is particuarly good-looking, I do find you rather attractive.
Awlrite darlen! Your mate's a right munter, but yooms evsa prittee.

By golly, you are a fine-looking hunk of a man.
Blige! Yoom an ansum basdurd.

If you would like to buy me a drink of quality cider I may be able to entertain you.
Get I a Blakforn an ee cas gif I a quicken.

Would you like to come back to my residence for a spot of light supper?
Fansy a pot nuda round at our muh's ows?

David, do not entertain this fool's penchant for violence.
Leebim Dave! Ee aint wurf it!

Kindly take your hands from me or I will be forced to take action.
Get off I, or I'll stick thee in the bleeden B R I.

By jove the music in this venue is awfully loud, don't you think?
Blige, I casn't yer nuffink in yer.

Do you think you could direct me to a residence where I may obtain light relief?
Do ee knows a good masarge parler rown yer?

I have to say that I was most entertained by the recent floor show I attended at the Colston Hall.
They strippers las night down the Colsnawl, they was gurt mint!

I find your physical appearance quite revolting.
Yoom a right macky munter.

Thank you
Churz

No thank you
Nah

I don't understand
What?

Good morning
Awlrite

Good afternoon
Awlrite

How are you
Awlrite

Good night
Churz en

Can you help me with…
Cas ee gif I an and wiv…

Could you please hold this for me?
Cas ee awd ee fry?

Can I have...
Canave...

Where did you get that?
Wheres gettee to?

Listen to that
Ark at ee

I just had to have it
I attle avit

Where have you been?
Wheres bin?

What is it you would like?
Whas want?

Excuse me...
Yer...

Do you speak English?
Whas on bout?

Where is it?
Wheres eetoo?

I am looking for…
Wheres eetoo…

Can you tell me…
Do ee know…

Good evening
Awlrite

Where are you?
Wheres eetoo?

Where are you going?
Wheres ee bleeden off to?

I say, is it you who has broken wind?
Ave ee guffed?

I am terribly sorry, what is it exactly that you are saying?
Whas ee chatbout?

Could you please give me change for this twenty pound note?
Cas ee gif I change of this twenny?

How are you?
Ow Bist?

The Official Bristolian Citizenship Test

So you want to move to Bristol do you? Of course you do, it rocks, we can totally understand that, but you know we do have standards. We can't just let in any old Jim, David, or Sunny – we have to keep our standards pretty high. So we're going to need you to pass our citizenship test before we can collect your rental deposit and fritter it away down the Grosvenor Casino.

Here are 24 questions pertaining to life in Bristol. Score 75 per cent or more and you're welcome to start rolling your Rs in any flat in Barton Hill. Less than that and you'll be living in a squat in Trowbridge.

1. The Bristol Pound can be spent at which of the following establishments?

☐ Tesco Express – Stokes Croft

☐ Aldi – Greystoke Avenue

☐ Middle-class quality independent retailers located in Southville or Gloucester Road.

☐ Any part of the Polski Sklep chain

2. Is the M Shed...

☐ Something that wasn't named properly

☐ My Shed with a letter missing

- [ ] A museum of Bristol located on the historic Harbourside
- [ ] A place where M People keep their lawnmower

3. The Bristol Hum is...

- [ ] The smell that emanates from the washing basket after your ole man has put his cacks in there
- [ ] The collective noise made by hippies meditating in their Redland bedsits
- [ ] A persistent and invasive low frequency humming noise heard by a small number of Bristolians
- [ ] An edgy musical fusion of drum and brass usually played by the Salvation Army

4. What is unique about the Mayor of Bristol, George Ferguson's, trousers?

- [ ] He doesn't wear any
- [ ] They are stuffed full of Bristol pounds
- [ ] They are red
- [ ] It's the wrong trousers Gromit and they've gone wrong!

5. The Bristol Post runs a front page story stating Bristol is getting a new tram system. Do you...

☐ Ignore it, you ride a bike, it is a cycling city after all.

☐ Immediately enter your registration at webuyanycar.com to sell your car

☐ Ignore it – they are short of stories again

☐ Start a lobby group to assess the environmental impact of the proposed scheme

6. Name the mythical creatures found at the Council House on College Green

☐ Red Dragons

☐ Value for money councillors

☐ Golden Unicorns

☐ The Chuckle Brothers

7. Archibald Leach was the real name of which actor from Bristol?

☐ Eddy 'I don't want to dance' Grant

☐ Russell 'I can read your horoscope' Grant

☐ Cary Grant

☐ Housing Grant

8. Which best-selling book was said to be the inspired by the Llandoger Trow pub?

☐ 50 Shades of Grey

☐ The Jungle Book

☐ Treasure Island

☐ A to Z of Cardiff

9. Which famous Cousins from Bristol won an Olympic Gold medal for Ice Skating?

☐ Ar muh's cousins

☐ Ar ole man's cousins

☐ Robin Cousins

☐ John Curry

10. Who is Brian Steel?

☐ International man of mystery

☐ Gloucestershire Cricket club's top batsman last season with an average of 7

☐ Some bloke who used to sell half-price suites, but now sells half-price carpets from his warehouse on the Fishponds Trading Estate

☐ Steel drummer with the 'The Caribbean Wurzels'

11. The Bristol Post runs a front page story stating Bristol is getting a new indoor arena. Do you...

☐ Ignore it as you are a Radio Bristol listener and therefore have no interest in modern music

☐ Start a lobby group to assess the environmental impact of the new arena

☐ Ignore it – they are short of stories again

☐ Start saving your money because those Acker Bilk tickets are never cheap

12. A stranger approaches you late and night and says "Awlrite me luvver?" Do you...

☐ Cross to the other side of the road pretending to be either deaf or foreign

☐ Quickly hand over your iPhone wailing "Not the face, please don't touch the face!"

☐ Simply reply "Not bad me babber, ow bist?"

☐ Immediately punch him in the face. He is clearly batting for the other side and any positive reaction could result in a leather-themed evening in the clubs of Old Market

Citizenship

13. Blue Lines was the 1991 debut album for which influential Bristol band?

☐ Massive Arrtack

☐ Mild Stroke

☐ Massive Attack

☐ Massive savings at the Gardiner Haskins sale

14. Who was Uncle Bruce?

☐ A film character played by John Candy

☐ A slightly sinister relative who used to bounce you on his knee while only dressed in his underpants

☐ A long-serving HTV News presenter

☐ A family friend always called Uncle despite the fact he clearly wasn't

15. Which Bristolian won the first series of Britain's Got Talent?

☐ Pol Pot

☐ Betty's Hot Pot

☐ Paul Potts

☐ Susan Boyle

16. What was the popular name given to the collection of anti-aircraft guns used in Bristol during the Second World War?

☐ The Gurt Greville Smyth Gun Club

☐ Paddy Pantsdown

☐ Purdown Percy

☐ Kickass Kev

17. Which long-running television drama left Bristol in 2012?

☐ Shoestring

☐ Catch Phrase (if you choose this it's good but it's not right)

☐ Casualty

☐ Come Dine Wiv I Me Babber

18. What was Bristol's most famous pirate son better known as?

☐ Blue Rinse Bert

☐ Somalia Steve

☐ Edward Blackbeard Teach

☐ Thermal Long Johns

19. The Latin motto of Bristol is Virtute et Industria —but what does this mean?

☐ All industry is virtually gone

☐ City of hopes, dreams, and kebab shops

☐ By Virtue and Industry

☐ Latin? I didn't go to Clifton College

20. Bristolian football legend Ian Holloway is famous for his quirky comments. Which of the following did he not say?

☐ Apparently it's my fault that the Titanic sank

☐ I couldn't be more chuffed if I were a badger at the start of the mating season

☐ My fellow Americans, ask not what your country can do for you, ask what you can do for your country

☐ I love Blackpool. We're very similar. We both look better in the dark

21. Which of the following song titles was a Wurzels classic depicting the lovely ladies of Bristol?

☐ Munters From The Mead

☐ Cider, Sunshine, and Scutlers

☐ Moonlight on the Malago

☐ Say Hi to Your Muh Fry Ullee?

22. Bristol Blue Glass gets its distinct colour from...

☐ Somebody dropping a biro into the mix

☐ Excessive swearing by glassblowers

☐ A combination of cobalt oxide and lead oxide

☐ Being really cold

23. The stuffed remains of which famous Alfred are on display at the Bristol Museum?

☐ Alfred the Butler from the slightly camp 1960s television series Batman and Robin

☐ Alfred the Great

☐ Alfred the Gorilla

☐ Alfred, ar muh's old dog

24. Which long-running BBC sitcom starring David Jason was filmed in Bristol?

☐ Allo Allo (I shall say this only once)

☐ Open All Hours

☐ Only Fools and Horses

☐ Crimewatch

Ark At Ee!

If you're stuck in Bristol's internationally renowned traffic and need something to pass the time, want to keep the kids occupied during the holidays, or just bored witless, then play our familiar Bristolian spotter game, Ark At Ee! Simply carry the book around with you and tick the box for all the items that you come across. If you manage to spot all the items, simply photocopy the pages as proof and post the copies to Noel Edmunds, c/o Deal or No Deal, Brislington.

Media

☐ Song played on BBC Radio Bristol produced after 1980

☐ Song played on Heart less than six times in one day

☐ Points West edition that didn't try to put a tenuous local spin on a national story

☐ Jack FM telling you they are playing what they want, otherwise known as a playlist

☐ Radio Bristol phone-in caller under 50 years old

☐ Article in the Bristol Post mostly made up of comments from Twitter or Facebook

☐ Somebody actually reading the Curtain Call section in the Bristol Observer

☐ Edition of the Bristol Observer that contained more than 15% news content

- [ ] Article in the Bristol Observer that was published in the Bristol Post the week before
- [ ] Someone laughing at one of Steve Yabsley's jokes
- [ ] Actual BBC Radio Bristol listener (football shows excluded)
- [ ] Article in the Bristol Post about Big Brother winner Josie Gibson's nan/boyfriend/toe nails
- [ ] Local television or radio presenter with even the slightest hint of a Bristolian accent

Sport

- [ ] Bristol football fan ringing Geoff Twentyman saying the manager should be sacked
- [ ] Runner in the Bristol 10K with more energy gels than you would need for a marathon
- [ ] Someone wearing big blue and white check shirt in The Robins, Ashton
- [ ] The moment it's accepted that Gloucestershire County Cricket Club are going to have another poor season (estimated to be around late April)
- [ ] Bristol Rugby Club making the Premiership
- [ ] Someone making a joke about the Bristol Academy Woman's football team swapping shirts

Ark At Ee!

Transport

- [ ] Any bus actually arriving on time
- [ ] Story in the Bristol Post about plans for a tram system in Bristol
- [ ] Cycle lane that isn't just red paint on the side of a road
- [ ] Bike rack in Broadmead without bike remnants still locked to it
- [ ] Cyclist riding around Bristol City centre on the road instead of the pavement
- [ ] Passenger on the bus ignoring the bell preferring to instead shout "Next stop drive"
- [ ] First actually reducing ticket prices rather than reviewing them

People

- [ ] Heather Small at the M Shed with a lawnmower
- [ ] George Ferguson in blue denim
- [ ] Avonmouth Mary
- [ ] Noel Edmunds playing at being a taxi driver to dodge traffic
- [ ] Ar Muh down Asdawl
- [ ] Any local MP outside of election time
- [ ] Wallace